These pages are one sided to prevent bleed through. As a precaution, please place a blank sheet of paper behind the page you are working on. This will help preserve your creation.

May you have many hours of stress-free fun!

Coloring Book Created by JoLea Studios